HANDS-ON
ASIA

ART ACTIVITIES FOR ALL AGES

FOLK ART OF ASIA

Asia is one of the world's richest regions for handcrafted textiles, carved wood, woven basketry, painted surfaces, costume and mask performance traditions, creative use of handmade paper and cherished toys and puppets. The Asian countries included here abound in fine art and craft traditions. Because Southeast Asia has experienced an enormous population loss with refugees settling in new areas throughout Europe and America, much of the art is enjoying respectful exposure to westerners.

This book is dedicated to Barbara Baugh,
a partner, a colleague in community service,
and a cherished friend.

Book design by Art & International Production, LLC
Laurel Casjens took the photographs
Mary Simpson illustrated the book and
assisted with the development of the crafts.

Other books by the author
from KITS Publishing:

Hands-on Alaska
(ISBN 0-9643177-3-7)

Hands-on Celebrations
(ISBN 0-9643177-4-5)

Hands-on Rocky Mountains
(ISBN 0-9643177-2-9)

Hands-on Latin America
(ISBN 0-9643177-1-0)

Hands-on Pioneers*
(ISBN 1-57345-085-5)

KITS PUBLISHING
2359 E. Bryan Avenue   Salt Lake City, Utah 84108
(801) 582-2517   fax: (801) 582-2540
e-mail - info@hands-on.com
*Published by Deseret Book

© 1999 Yvonne Young Merrill
First printing May, 1999
Printed in China

Library of Congress Catalog Number 98-75297

ISBN 0-9643177-5-3

HANDS-ON ASIA

ART ACTIVITIES FOR ALL AGES

YVONNE Y. MERRILL

KITS PUBLISHING

TABLE OF CONTENTS

AN OVERVIEW OF THE FAITHS OF ASIA

The beliefs of the varied people of Asia have formed their rich cultures. Many features of the cultures are reflected in their arts such as traditional dances, ancient musical instruments, theater performances that are centuries old, and the fine arts. An overview of four main faiths will enhance an understanding of Asian values as they are reflected in the activities in this book.

BUDDHISM

In about 356 B.C. Siddhartha Gautama, a prince in India, traveled for six years in search of wisdom. In a vision one night his mind saw a vision of his past lives and life's deeper meanings. That day he became Buddha, which means "the enlightened one." Buddha taught that suffering comes from wanting things. By following the Middle Way one can overcome these desires. Buddhists believe there is no individual soul or self, people are born again and again until they reach Nirvana, a perfect harmony with all things. Buddhists believe in treating all living things with respect.

CONFUCIANISM

Born in China around 500 B.C., Confucius saw bad behavior in local rulers. He studied philosophies of the past and then traveled the land, telling people his ideas: people should be kind to their neighbors, honor their parents, respect their leaders and control their tempers. Everyone should be educated in the arts. He soon had many followers who gathered his thoughts into books. Great temples have been built honoring him where rituals of dance, music and sacrifices are performed.

HINDUISM

Over three thousand years ago, a wandering Aryan tribe settled on the banks of the Indus River and told stories of many gods. The gods came to earth in a disguise to help people. Vishnu came as a fish to warn of a flood, Rama battled demons, Krishna helped warriors in battle. All these gods were part of Brahman, the spirit of the universe. Their knowledge was passed down in writings known as Vedas. Hindus believe that souls are born over and over until they reach perfection. Most Hindu homes have a family shrine where the faithful pray everyday. Hindu meditation opens their minds and hearts to God.

SHINTOISM

In the beginning of time, the world was a large egg which then divided into many pieces which became known as *kami* or gods. The kami had supernatural powers to bless human lives. Later it was believed that the emperor was descended from the sun. Many shrines were built to please the kami and honor the emperor. After World War II Shintoism became a religion of the people instead of emperor-worship. Shinto means "way of the gods" and teaches followers to care about this world...not a hereafter. Passages in life are celebrated: births, etc. At important festivals small shrines are carried to bless the homes it passes.

IMPORTANT POINTS OF INTEREST

1. Japan
Great Buddha Hall

2. Lhasa
Potola Palace

3. Indonesia
Komodo Lizard

4. China
Long Men Caves

5. China
The Great Wall

6. China
Hong Kong

7. Japan
Buddha at Kamakura

8. Thailand
Elephant Round Up

9. Indonesia
Batik Expert

10. China
Panda Bear

11. Thailand
Chang Mai Wood Carver

12. China
Tiananmen Square and
The Forbidden City

13. Nepal
Mt. Everest

14. Japan
I.M. Pei building

15. China
Xian Warriors

16. Mongolia
The Gobi Desert

17. Cambodia
Angkor Wat

18. Malaysia
Batu Caves

19. Japan
Mt. Fuji

20. Java
Borobudur

MAP OF ASIA & INDONESIA

JAPANESE FOLK ART

Japanese art is one of the world's great cultural legacies. Bonsai plant designs, packaging as an art form, papermaking, and folk art toy production are just a few that show a continuing emphasis on traditional objects. Artists and artisans have important status in Japanese culture.

JAPANESE FOLK ART

Hokkaido →

Sea of Japan

Kobe

Nagasaki

Tokyo

Kyoto

Japan is a string of islands in the Pacific Ocean off the coast of Asia. During the Ice Age (22,000 years ago) the northern and southern tips of Japan were connected to the continent. By 1300 B.C. trade routes by land and river were introducing new materials. By 500 B.C. the potter's wheel helped create Japan's oldest craft tradition. Bronze tools made life easier, too. People lived off the sea or rivers, as they still do.

HANIWA BURIAL OBJECTS: In the fifth century villages were ruled by shamans or chiefs. When these important people were buried, the burial mounds contained clay figures called *haniwa*. These were small molded objects that accompanied the body in death. They represented the earthly life of the deceased and were often a house, horse, servant, pet, etc. This may have been the earliest craft form in Japan's rich tradition. Certain forms became symbols of luck such as the horse, rabbit, cat, etc.

ANIMISM, JAPAN'S ANCIENT RELIGION: Another influence in Japan's artistic expression is the ancient beliefs of "Animism" a religion in which spirits of nature are of main importance. Many examples of today's folk art are animistic in origin. Japanese art reflects the reverence for plant life, water forms, sky elements and all natural creations. The simplicity of nature is another prevailing theme in Japanese art.

SHINTOISM: THE OLDEST RELIGION STILL PRACTICED IN JAPAN. Based on the worship of nature, Shintoism is only practiced in Japan. It is believed that divine spirits, called *kami* live in the wind, rain, mountains, forests, fields and waterfalls. The highest priest was the emperor. Japan has always had an emperor and a military leader called a Shogun.

BUDDHISM: The Buddhist religion began in India and spread through China to Japan. With Buddhism came the Sutra, which contained Buddha's teachings and Chinese writing, which Japanese strove to adapt to their own language. The Indian **BUDDHA** has several hands as a sign of superhuman powers. Two of the hands are usually pressed together in prayer. The jewel in the middle of the forehead represents the "third eye of wisdom." Long earlobes symbolize Buddha's royal birth. The lotus is the flower of Buddha. The name Buddha means "Enlightened One." The Japanese Great Buddha as seen at Kamakura was created in the 1200s and presents Buddha with just two arms. This is typical of all Japanese Buddhas.

ZEN is a sect of Buddhism that emphasizes simple living and worships no images.

All of these religious traditions have marked Japanese folk crafts and fine art.

Japanese Pagoda

FOLK ART FLOURISHES: Edo is the old name for modern Tokyo. During the Edo period, the 13th to 16th century, art flourished because peace and plenty allowed common people to become prosperous enough to create an art of their own. They crafted their houses, made pots, carved boxes, wove cloth and baskets, all of which were in harmony with their daily lives. Once these hand crafted treasures could be found all over Japan. Today they survive in a few isolated villages.

Specific folk toys have traditionally come from certain regions. Some of the toy forms and materials can be traced to the burial object, *haniwa*. Folk toys, however, are not traditional playthings. Their primary purpose was to serve as amulets, souvenirs and charms, capable of granting wishes and avoiding evil. This rich symbolism and magical meaning attached to folk toys is not strange in a country where the strong foundation is Shinto animism which still pervades many aspects of daily life. The *wara-uma* (straw horse) was supposed to carry the god *Doso-jim* on his back when he visited mankind to disperse prosperity.

The earth, tree and plants are homes of the *kami* and when made into forms of clay, straw, and wood represent the deities and are believed to have their curative and protective powers. The underlying spirit is described as *shibui:* austere, subtle and subdued.

Regions throughout the islands were known for specific folk craft skills. Cultural and artistic exchanges occurred with the building of the great Tokaido road between Edo (Tokyo) and Kyoto. Common qualities came to identify many folk pieces. Happily various folk toys have survived in their primary form. A small number have stayed true to their origins while others were "modernized" for commercial purposes. Some bear no resemblance to the originals. Still the cultural meanings continue:

Daruma dolls   good luck images

Specific toy-amulets protect against hysteria, melon thieves, fire, clogged noses and earthquake. Others give health, wealth, happiness, safe journeys, luck in business, good marriage partners, and abundant silkworm harvest...though the luck is valid for only one year.

POTTERY: Tea masters prized tea vessels that were beautifully crafted. 400 years ago the making of tea pots, cups, dishes and trays was the true beginning of folk art. The emphasis was not only on beautiful pieces *but on their actual use.* Deep interest developed in objects of industrial use as well. The anonymity of the objects, their simplicity and spontaneity evolved to the Japanese "religion of beauty" we know today.

BASKETRY is of grass, bamboo, bark and branches. Next to pottery, the most popular of the folk arts is basketry. Archeological remains from prehistoric Japan indicate that basketry was fully developed some 3000 years ago. Headwear, woven boots, capes, trays, and containers of every type and use are part of basketry.

MASKS AND THEATER have been performed for 600 years. The No drama had early beginnings in the farmer's festivals. Kabuki, the national theater, originated with early folk tales woven into literary classics.

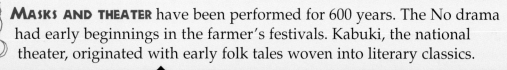

KABUKI WARRIOR MASK

KABUKI WARRIOR MASK

Materials: a white paper plate of any size, red and white tempera paint, black railroad board, black and red marker, stapler, scissors, glue, pencil, string for wearing the mask.

1. Measure and mark the middle of the plate with light pencil across and up and down. Mark the nose place, 3/4 inch above the middle cross (A). Fold a heavy piece of white paper 4 x 3 inches and draw a half a nose with tabs for inserting into the mask. Cut out the nose and insert the tabs into the carefully measured tab slots.

2. Lightly pencil in the eyes. Check their placement by wearing the mask. Carefully cut out the eye slits.

3. With your pencil, mark the **symmetrical** patterns on the plate. To insure this balance cut out scrap paper stencils that you trace around (B). Draw the eyelines and descriptive mouth that give your mask the Japanese warrior expression. Now paint or marker in the black and red designs you have created.

4. If your white plate is now smudged, paint with white tempera to give it a white chalk make up appearance. The Kabuki mask was stark white.

5. Cut a pattern for the black extension pieces. Draw 8 of the shapes on your black railroad board. Cut them out. Make two for the top that are smaller (C).

6. Make the forehead piece by cutting a half circle 6 x 4 inches. Cut 2 notches in the straight edge, overlapping and stapling to create a curved piece (D). Glue or staple the black "arms" to the mask, making sure they line up on each side. Glue or staple on the curved forehead piece. Add the string at the ear marks and try on your mask.

This *Kabuki* warrior figure has not changed in makeup or appearance since his first appearance in 1729. He is named *Goro*. The play opens with his sharpening arrowheads. His fantastic head-piece has been a popular theme for posters, advertising imagery, greeting cards, etc.

JAPANESE GOOD LUCK TOYS

JAPANESE GOOD LUCK TOYS

DARUMA DOLLS AND WELCOMING CAT

Materials: any size plastic separating eggs, masking tape, a few pebbles for nesting in the egg bottom, a small-tipped brush, acrylic or tempera paint of white, flesh, red, black etc., a fine-tipped marker or pencil, spray paint or gold markers are optional.

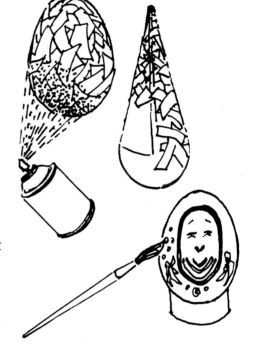

1. Place the pebbles in the base of the fattest egg half. Tape a piece of masking tape over them to hold in place. Assemble the egg and see if it balances, wobbles or tips. Adjust the pebbles so it balances.

2. Cover the egg with 1 to 2 inch pieces of masking tape. (If you are adding the cone hat, tape on two triangles adjusting until the cone is sharp. Cover the triangles with tape.)

3. Paint the taped egg with tempera, acrylic or spray paint. Make a paper ring and rest your daruma on it to dry.

4. Draw the face of the daruma with a pencil. Paint it with white or flesh-colored paint. After it has dried, pencil in the features. Traditionally, one or both of the eyes are left blank. When your wish comes true the eye is drawn on the daruma.

The good luck Welcoming Cat activity is on page 76.

The name *Daruma* comes from Sanskrit *Dharma*. It represents a monk who sat in meditation for so long that his arms and legs fell off. But, because of his spiritual enlightenment, he was even more stable than before and always remained upright when tilted.

The round-faced daruma represents Emperor Ojin when he was a child. He is wrapped in his protective red clothing. Since the 1700s this daruma has been given to newly wed couples as a hope for a healthy baby. It has also been given to sick people to encourage recovery. Another daruma tradition occurs at New Years when the dolls are thrown into yards and the open front doors of friends. The weighted toy immediately returns to its upright position symbolizing a quick recovery from any mishap during the coming year. The conical hat daruma represents the farmers of Niigata prefecture as a joke on themselves. They make their conical hats out of cypress trees.

TWO ASIAN KITES

TWO ASIAN KITES

A JAPANESE YAKKO KITE

Materials: the pattern for coloring is on page 81, scissors, markers or crayons, two red plastic stirrers, tape, string, one-inch cut strips from a plastic garbage bag.

1. This traditional kite with a warrior figure is made from an 8 1/2 inch x 11 inch piece of colored paper. You may wish to enlarge it on a copy machine. Increase the plastic tails and backside plastic supports accordingly.

2. Cut out the kite and color it. Traditional colors are black, red, white and blue.

3. Cross the two stirrers at the place indicated on the back of the colored cutout.

4. Tie the string to the crossing place.

5. Cut the one inch strips from the plastic bag at least 3 1/2 to 4 feet long. Tape them to the base.

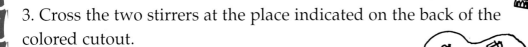

THAI KITE

Materials: a 12 inch square of any colored art paper, crepe paper or any choice for tail strips, a light but sturdy piece of wood, dowel or bamboo for kite form, tape, string, pencil, ruler, printed kite paper or markers for decorating.

1. Turn the decorated square paper front down and fold back inward on dotted lines.

2. Place reed down the back center and tape in place. Arch reed in back and tape in place.

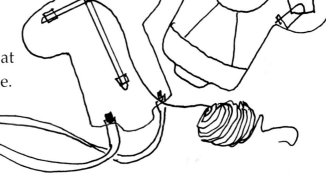

3. Your kite back should look like this. Turn the kite over and attach bridle string to these points. Add four tails.

The Yakko kite comes from the early Edo period when an accidentally overturned oil lamp could destroy the flimsy wood and paper homes. The kite symbolically cuts through the wind and so reduces its power to fan the flames. The kite is sold on New Year's Day, clearing the path for good luck as the yakko, the servant, did for his master.

JAPANESE TWIG VASE &
CARVED VEGIES

JAPANESE TWIG VASE & CARVED VEGIES

Materials: 1 soup can, emptied and cleaned, 1/8 inch thick twigs: 2 twigs cut 18 inches long, 35 straight twigs 6-7 inches long, sawed or cut from a bush such as bridal wreath or forsythia, 2 rubber bands, raffia, twine, ribbon or rope, a serrated bread knife or a sturdy pruning tool.

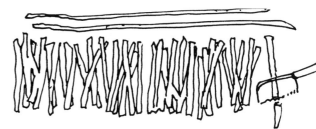

1. Choose your bush by examining the longest branches. After stripping the leaves check that the branch is quite straight so the diameter is half your little finger in width. Is it the color you like? Cut or saw about 10 branches that will be workable.

2. Using a cut 6-7 inch twig, lay it against the stripped branches and mark the lengths for your twigs. Using a protective surface such as a rolled newspaper, carefully saw, or cut with strong pruning shears, your 35 twigs (they do not have to be perfect in length. This is your aesthetic decision). You now have your two 18 inch long handle twigs cut and your 35 short twigs.

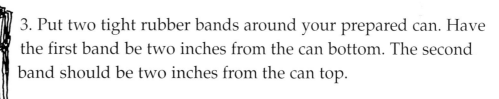

3. Put two tight rubber bands around your prepared can. Have the first band be two inches from the can bottom. The second band should be two inches from the can top.

4. Push each twig under the two rubber bands, lining them up side by side, close and touching. Insert the twisted pair of handle twigs when it looks as though you are half way around the container. After you have placed your twigs and handle allow a couple of days for everything to dry. You will probably have to add one or two more twigs due to shrinkage.

5. Wrap your decorative material around the two rubber bands and a third near the top of your twig vase.

Creative Vegies continued on page 78.

CLAY SLAB PLATE

CLAY SLAB DISH

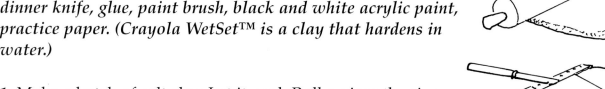

Materials: a recipe for cooked salt clay on page 79, a rolling pin, a non-stick flat surface, a 4 x 5 inch paper pattern, a ruler, dinner knife, glue, paint brush, black and white acrylic paint, practice paper. (Crayola WetSet™ is a clay that hardens in water.)

1. Make a batch of salt clay. Let it cool. Roll a piece the size of a grapefruit out to 1/4 inch thickness.

2. Using your ruler as a guide measure and cut out a rectangle 4 x 5 1/2 inches. Cut 2 clay feet 3 1/2 inches long and 1/2 inch thick.

3. Put the clay rectangle on a nonstick surface and curl up each corner. Support the upturned corners with paper wads until clay is dry. The salt clay dries slooooooowly. Placing the dish and feet in a slightly heated oven overnight will speed the process.

4. When clay parts are dry attach the feet to the dish with glue.

5. Paint the slab dish a color and allow it to dry (we painted ours white).

6. Choose the calligraphied message from one of the characters below. These are commonly used to decorate stone, metal, cloth and clay objects. Practice your calligraphy on paper until you are ready to brush it on your plate.

7. Here are more ideas for making a rolled clay (slab) project. Commercial self-hardening clay will work well. Try a fish plate, a leaf plate, or a plate with a shallow rim. They are all traditionally Asian.

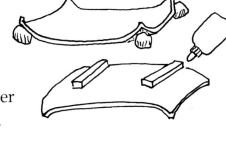

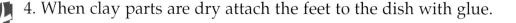
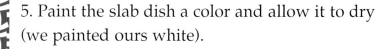
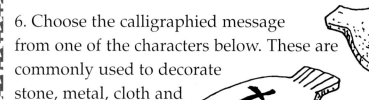

kindness   peace   good luck

仁　平　吉

happiness   love

喜　愛

Pottery is Japan's most popular and developed folk craft. Each painted flower design has a special meaning: peonies mean spring, flowering plums symbolize winter, the lotus (the sacred flower of Buddha) is summer and the chrysanthemum represents fall.

TWO JAPANESE NO MASKS

TWO JAPANESE NO MASKS
Saru, the Monkey Mask

Materials: a manila file folder, a fistful of natural raffia, ruler, scissors, sponges, washable paint: red and brown markers or orange, black, red and brown, glue and a hole punch. String for wearing the mask.

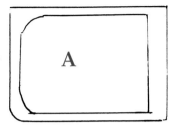 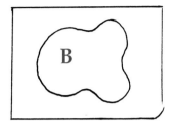

The old man No mask instructions are continued on page 77.

1. Mark and cut a U-shape, 6 x 9 inches from one side of the folder (piece A). Cut a face shape as shown that is 5 x 5 inches (piece B). Make brown scratch marks 2-3 inches long from the edge of piece A. Using a damp sponge, dab brownish paint over the marks.

2. Pencil in the monkey face on piece B, dividing the face into thirds: the mouth and cheek line (a), the nose, the second third (b) and the circled eyes the top third. Color in the marker lines. With the rinsed, damp sponge corner dab reddish around the mouth and reddish-brown around the cheeks. Dab beige on the eye section.

3. Glue the finished, dry face onto the prepared A piece. Punch about 10 holes at the top of Piece A, 5 on each side.

4. Separate from the natural raffia about 5 folded-in the-middle strands. They should be uneven lengths. Insert the raffia bunch into each hole, front to back so the hairy strands come from the mask front. Coat the back side with glue to secure the raffia bunches. Punch holes in the eye places (two thicknesses) and in the mask edges at the ear place. Tie string to each ear place and try on the mask.

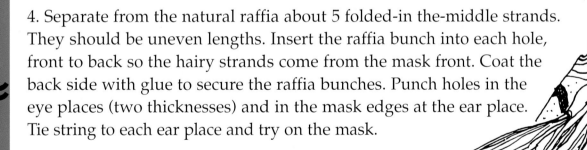

The earliest No dramas were performed 600 years ago. The nobility and samurai attended the near-sacred productions. It is only in recent times that the public has seen the plays. The No stage has not changed: four pillars mark the stage, there is a chorus, the two main characters are *Shite* **and Waki.** Waki tells the story, comments on the plot and often explains it to the audience. He even mediates with the gods. Performances are usually a day-long event. The Kyogen comedy acts break up the scenes.

JAPANESE SAMURAI ARMOR

JAPANESE SAMURAI ARMOR

Materials: red railroad board, 22 x 28 inches, black tempera paint, black railroad board, aluminum from a disposable baking pan, a carrot and potato for printing the designs, a hole punch, string, stapler, scissors, glue, pencil.

1. Lay out your railroad board and cut pieces a,b,c,d,e,f from the dimensions of the parts drawn:
   a. the 2 shoulder straps (red)
   b. the 4 armor horizontal pieces (red)
   c. the 3 curved neck protectors for helmet (red)
   d. the back armor piece attached to the shoulder straps (red)
   e. the 2 front pieces for helmet (red)
   f. the helmet cap circle (black)

2. Cut out the black cardboard helmet. Score the areas for folding. Fold over the center and two side pieces and staple them as they overlap (g).

3. Cut the edges of the red helmet neck protectors so they will curve (h).

4. Paint the black designs dipping a carrot end in black paint, on a paper plate, and the straight ridge cut from a potato. Stamp the designs on the 3 curved back helmet pieces (h) and the 4 horizontal armor pieces (i).

5. Staple the 2 curved side sections (e) before you glue the red neck pieces to the black helmet. Add the silver horn piece to the visor (j).

6. Assemble the breastplate armor by overlapping from the bottom to the top, after you have done the carrot and potato printing. String the armor through the holes you have punched. Add the strap to fit and the decorated back plate, attaching the shoulder straps with string to the front and back plates. Try on your armor. Try your helmet for a good fit.

The Samurai were Japan's military aristocracy. The Age of Battles or Warring States period from 1550 to 1600 was their high point. It was generally a class to be born or legally adopted into.

BENTO: THE JAPANESE LUNCHBOX

BENTO: THE JAPANESE LUNCHBOX

Materials: a square or rectangular-lidded Styrofoam food container, scissors, planning paper, pencil, markers, crayons, etc. for decorating the bento.

1. **Mask Bento:** Plan the mask face. This book presents an Edo period woman, a Kabuki actor, and two No masks. Refer to these for help. Decorate the container lid with markers or acrylic paint. Glue on the paper headwear.

2. **Daruma Bento:** Look at the Daruma faces in the book. Pencil the face on the lid container. Decorate the face with marker or paint. Draw in an empty eye to be filled in later for good luck.

3. **Animal Bento:** Many animals can be designed on the empty lid. The photo shows the crab. Here is a fish idea. Glue on details such as fish fins, crab legs, etc.

4. **Wrapped Bento:** Following the printmaking instructions on page 33, print paper with Japanese symbols. Consider bamboo stalks and leaves, fish, circles, and waves. Potato cut shapes and brushed on tempera paint will make a nice print. After the gift paper has dried wrap your packed container and tie with string.

Ekiben **is the name for the extraordinary cold box lunches available at train stations** all over Japan. *Ekiben* **is like our fast food. Containers are extravagantly decorated to describe the food inside (a crab on the lid of crab-filled sushi is an example). The lid may also represent a local symbol. The Bento box is a lunchbox used by everyone. The Japanese traditionally put as much effort into the presentation of the food as the taste and nutritional value.**

JAPANESE STICK PUPPETS AND SHINTO BIRD

JAPANESE STICK PUPPETS
AND THE SHINTO BIRD

Materials: the cooked salt dough recipe on page 79, a craft stick for each puppet, a walnut-size roll of dough per puppet head, a fine-tipped brush, all colors of acrylic or tempera paint, a small container of water, a pencil.

1. There are many figures in the traditional puppet theater: the fox (usually red), the cat (often yellow), the white-faced head, the mean face, the sweet face. As you stick your roll of dough atop your craft stick, think about the puppets you will make.

2. Dip your fingers into the water and mold the faces with big noses, peaked hairdos and hats, fat hair sides or ear pieces. These puppets can make you laugh!!

3. Plan on 12-18 hours for the puppet heads to dry. Paint them when they are dry. Mark the facial features with a pencil. Paint them bright and happy colors. Design a wearable puppet theater out of a box that looks like this. The traditional puppeteer was as beloved and common in Asian children's neighborhoods as the American ice cream man.

The Shinto Bird activity is on page 80.

These heads are called *Ichironsan* and are as old as the Edo period. The story is told of the greengrocer, Mr. Ichiron, making them to earn extra money. He stuck them on bamboo and sold them in his shop. Eventually they became so popular that their production became a cottage industry that has lasted to this day. They are the heads of warriors, mythical beings, folk heroes and famous actors.

EASY PRINTMAKING

EASY PRINTMAKING

Materials: a Styrofoam meat tray, scissors, paper, pencil, felt-tipped marker, engraving tools such as a nail or toothpick, plastic straw, spoon, fork, water-based ink or tempera paint, brayer, cookie sheet.

1. Look and think about a simple design from nature such as a fish, a flower, a bird, a leaf, etc. Make several sketches until a simple shape emerges.

2. To make a printing block, cut a smooth center area from the Styrofoam tray.

3. Using paper and pencil draw the design for printing from your practice sketches. Lightly redraw with a soft marker on a Styrofoam block. Don't press hard.

4. Now make the design into foam with tools: make punctures with a nail-end, curves with a plastic piece etc. These will all make interesting printed patterns. Any mark incised in your block will not be inked. Do not press too hard. **Do not puncture through the Styrofoam surface.**

5. Spread ink or paint onto a cookie sheet and roll smoothly onto a brayer. If a brayer is unavailable brush the ink onto your print surface. Roll brayer over the block to ink it. Make a test print. Place paper carefully over the inked block. Rub paper with spoon back or clean hand. To check if your print has enough ink lift the corner of the paper while holding down the rest. Now you can make more patterns in your design, add more ink and try another print.
Do not smudge or move your print.

6. When print results are good make many prints with different kinds of paper and colors of paint or ink. Try making a Japanese lantern following the drawn instructions.

In 251 A.D. in China, Wei Tan developed ink from soot and glue. Ink and the previously invented paper led to woodblock printing. Prints were made in China and Japan by 750 A.D.

CHINESE, TIBETAN, MONGOLIA & KOREAN FOLK ART

Each culture has influenced the other as skills have evolved through centuries of remarkable traditions. Embroidered silk has become embroidered hides and art weavings in Tibet. Korean clothing, jewelry and toys are unique to the culture but bear a resemblance to China's similar objects. Each culture continues to prize forms that ward off evil as did the masks, good luck omens, colors and symbols from early beliefs.

CHINA, KOREA, TIBET, AND MONGOLIA

China was a flourishing culture long before the classical Greeks had begun their influence. China was a huge country, stretching over 1800 miles. The land resembles three steps in a staircase, descending from west to east: the highest step in the Tibetan plateau where the Yellow and the Yangtze rivers originate. The forests and deserts of central China and finally the coast. Chinese civilizations began around the Yellow River where the soil is a rich earth called *loess*. By 2700 B.C. people were skilled at crafts and farming with bronze tools. During the Shang Dynasty, 1500 B.C., there is the gradual appearance of writing. Bronze tools were decorated with mythological animals. These symbols prevailed throughout the history of China.

jade "bi" disc   the serpent   the dragon   yin/yang

The Yin-Yang remains the best known Chinese symbol today. It is used throughout China to counteract evil. Most country homes have the yin-yang above their doors. The yin, the female element, represents the heart. The yang, the male element, represents heaven, sun and light.

By 356 B.C. the Chinese had a written language, weaving, pottery, bronze casts and jade carvings and needles for sewing. They understood the principles of astronomy and had a calendar. They invented printing and had an encyclopedia as early as 1005 A.D.

In 712, Hsuan-tsung came to power, one of China's greatest emperors. In his forty-two year reign, arts and crafts flourished. The Chinese had a clear distinction between arts and crafts. Painting, poetry and calligraphy were considered art and other skills were crafts.

The famous Silk Road allowed China to get silk to European markets for hundreds of years. The Ancient Greeks wrote about silk carriers called serers.

NEPAL

Bordering India, this country of Himalayan mountains is a destination for trekkers and climbers asending Mt. Everest, the highest peak in the world. Nepalese live similarly to people of Mongolia, grazing animals on high plateaus and living nomadic lifestyles.

KOREA

Today Korea is two political units: The Democratic People's Republic of Korea (North Korea) and the Republic of Korea (South Korea). The history of Korea began with the land called "Choson" meaning "The Land of the Morning Calm". The Three Kingdom period, first century B.C. is the first recorded history. Buddhism from China was introduced at this time. In 668 A.D.the kingdoms were unified by Silla who was over-thrown by Koryo in 935. The great Choson Dynasty from 1392 to 1910 established Seoul as its capital. During all of this period there is a clear influence of the Chinese culture. It is evident in Buddhist art, music, a written language and Confucianism. Korean dress was also affected by Chinese influence and the Mongols.

perfume pouches   a fur cap

shoes

Embroidered symbols were evident on most decorative items: sun, rock, cloud, bamboo, water, pine tree, mushroom of immortality, crane, turtle and deer.

TIBET

The size of Tibet is 6 times the size of Texas. It is called the "Roof of the World"at 14,000 ft. elevation. Tibet is the most inaccessible Asian country. By the end of the sixth century Tibet was a loose feudal confederation of nomads and shepherds. The greatest king was Tsan-Gam Po who gave the people their written language. He had two wives: one from Nepal and one from China. Buddhism was introduced to Tibet through the wives. A shaman-based faith called "Bon" also prevailed.

MONGOLIA

Mongolians live in the heart of the Asian continent. They raise and train strong horses. They live in moveable houses made of wood and covered with felt called "yurts" or *gers*. They believe their human spirit is connected to the land and the animals. The Mongol Empire was one of the great land empires in history under Genghis Khan. In the 12th century Kublai Khan, his grandson, first introduced China to Europe and the early trade routes were developed. It was Kublai Khan that Marco Polo visited.

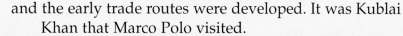

NEPAL SNOW LEOPARD MASK

NEPAL SNOW LEOPARD MASK

Materials: A craft paper 10 x 24 inches, pencil, stapler, scissors, glue, yarn, markers or crayon, paper scraps and tissue paper. The pattern is on page 78.

1. Fold the long piece of craft paper so it is 3 thicknesses. Staple the bottom. Adjust the band after fitting it around the head, allowing for a 2-3-inch overlap. Fold the paper in half to determine the center.

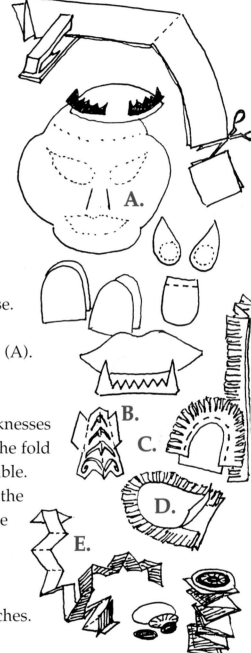

2. Using the pattern on page 78 cut the leopard shape. Choosing contrasting colored paper mark and cut out the eyes, double ears and tongue, teeth and mouth. Decorate each feature with colored paper and black marker accents.

The nose: Fold a contrasting piece of heavy paper down the middle. Draw a half nose with tabs for inserting into your mask. Cut it out so when you open the folded paper you have a 3 dimensional nose. Make bright patterns with your markers. Carefully mark the tabs lining up the nose in the mask middle (A). Cut the tab marks and insert the nose (B).

The fringed ears: Cut tissue paper that is 3 to 4 thicknesses and 10 x 2 inches. Cut fringe 1/8 inch apart. Cut to the fold but not through it. You should have ears that are double. Glue or staple the fringe around the outside edge of the bottom ear (C). Glue the top ear directly on top of the fringed bottom ear (D). Glue to the back top of the mask.

The pop-ups: Cut 2 bright strips of paper 1/2 x 6 inches. Fold over and under making the strong leg for the decorated circle (E). Make several of these, but know where you want to place them. Decorate the end circles and glue the pop-ups to the mask.

The nostril yarn fringe and tissue paper chin fringe are optional. They add a nice cat touch.

The elusive snow leopard image appears in the illustrated lore of Nepal, Tibet and other mountainous Asian cultures. The cat is appliqued on children's clothing and painted on toys as an omen of protection.

CHINESE HAND DRUM

CHINESE HAND DRUM

Materials: 2 <u>metal</u> lids (not canning jar rings, the tops must be solid metal), at least 3 inches wide, as close to the same width as possible, a wooden craft stick, 2 bells, any size, masking tape, red acrylic paint (spray or brush-on), fine-tipped brush, black marker, acrylic or tempera paint: green, yellow, red, 12 inches of yarn or string.

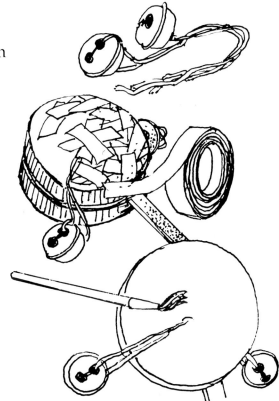

1. String the two bells on their separate string halves. Each string should be 2 1/2 to 3 inches in length when doubled.

2. Put the two lids together at the rims so there is a hollow inside space. Insert the stick and secure it with masking tape.

3. Cover the lids with torn masking tape pieces, securing each yarn end at the center on each side of the lid. Reinforce the stick and the yarn ends as the masking tape pieces are applied. When finished the drum can be tested by twisting the stick. The bells should strike the metal lid surfaces and make a ping sound on their opposite side. Practice seeing how rapidly you can make the bells hit.

4. Now the drum is ready for painting and decorative sides. Paint the drum red, either spray paint it or brush on acrylic paint. When it has dried, mark the 1 1/2 inch circle and paint with yellow. Marker or paint this drawn design using this template. Add symbols around the edge if you wish.

Here are some traditional Chinese circle designs

Music or bells are believed to calm the mind and aid thought. On hearing a piece of ritual music, Confucius was inspired to reject worldly comforts. He thought music was almost as necessary as food. An orchestra played at the royal palace whenever there was a banquet or when the emperor had guests. Usually the musicians were women.

KOREAN WRAPPER & PENDANT

KOREAN WRAPPER & PENDANT

Materials: Pastel colors of tissue paper (no fewer than six), glue, scissors, ruler, 1 bottom tissue paper 18"x 18", pencil, plain school craft paper. Pendant materials: 1 main color of tissue paper 6" x 15", file folder, fine-tipped markers, scissors and glue.

Making a Pojagi (sheer wrapping cloth):

1. Using a pencil, a ruler and some school craft paper design your triangle shapes for your "quilt" in size and spacing on your practice paper.

2. Cut out the colored tissue papers exactly and place them on top of the design plan. Make sure they are all the same size, that two triangles make a square and that the border is even.

3. Glue the edges together. Glue on the four-sided border strips. Glue the bottom tissue piece to the quilted top. Glue a ribbon or paper loop to the middle.

Making the Norigae (decorative pendants):

1. Using a pattern you have cut from paper trace around the shape and make 4-5 exact copies from the file folder cardboard. Decorate them with markers.

2. Cut the 6 inch fringe from rolled strips of tissue paper 8"x 15". Cut tiny strips so the paper looks like a shredded pom-pom. With a long strip of same-color paper connect the small decals. Glue this strip into the paper tassel that has been wrapped with paper.

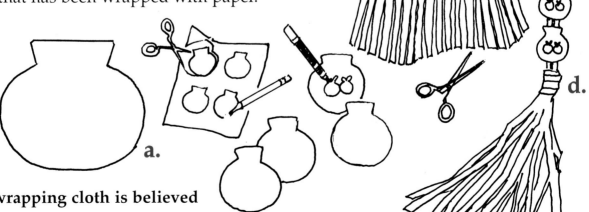

The pojagi wrapping cloth is believed to trap "pok" or Happiness inside the cloth layers. The pojagi were used to cover food and originally had an oiled paper lining. The embroidered pojagis were used to wrap wedding gifts. The norigaes were worn hanging from belts. Jade norigae were worn in summer to ward off the heat. Winter norigaes had pouches as Korean robes did not have pockets.

TIBETAN JEWELRY

TIBETAN JEWELRY

Materials: an aluminum pizza pan at least 12 inches round, scissors, a blunt point such as a pencil or nail point (for embossing the aluminum) 6-8 washers, yarn, cording for wearing around the neck. Earrings are made from the same foil.

1. Fold a newspaper or big piece of scrap paper. Draw the shape of the necklace on half the paper. Cut it out using the fold to create the matching half.

2. Lay the paper necklace pattern on the pizza pan. Trace around the shape with a pencil point. Cut out any additional decorative pieces.

3. Draw some designs to emboss on the silver surface. The technique is called repousse' and is the method used for beautifying real silver Tibetan jewelry.

4. Transfer the design ideas from the paper to the cut out aluminum pieces using your nail or pencil point to press the patterns. Work on a surface softened with newspaper layers or layers of paper towel so there is cushioning.

5. Measure at 2 inch intervals and gently punch a hole at the base of the bowed necklace. Paper clip, sew or wire the dangling washer circles. Glue or staple the silver rays.

6. Again gently punch a hole at the top of each "horn" and insert the two knotted ends of a cord for hanging the piece around the neck.

Tibetan refugees left their homeland wearing their wealth and art, much of it in stunning jewelry rich in repousse´ (pressing the design onto the metal surface) and encrusted stones. Turquoise is the favorite jewel of Tibetan women. The horns on this necklace represent the deer antlers, a popular motif in Tibetan art.

仁
吉
平

CHINESE CALLIGRAPHY SCROLL

Materials: a 1 inch pointed brush (a sumi brush is ideal), scrap paper for practice, black ink, high quality paper 7 x 14 inches for writing, colored paper 11 x 19 inches for mounting, two strips of black wood, 11 inches each (chopsticks work well), glue and string.

1. Practice holding your brush in the traditional position, straight up, supported on one side with the thumb, on the opposite side with the index finger, third finger in front and fourth finger in back.

2. Dip the tip of your brush into the ink and experiment with strokes. Only the tip of your brush is to be used for writing. To make thin strokes, use only the very tip. To make broader strokes press down.

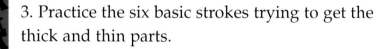

3. Practice the six basic strokes trying to get the thick and thin parts.

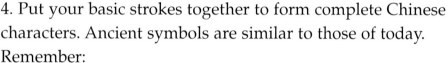

4. Put your basic strokes together to form complete Chinese characters. Ancient symbols are similar to those of today. Remember:

* Strokes are drawn in order from top to bottom
* from left to right
* from outside to inside
* horizontal first then vertical
* slanting left strokes then slanting right

All characters occupy an imaginary square.

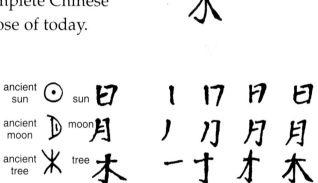

5. Choose the characters you wish to present for your scroll. Plan an equal imaginary square space for each character. Lightly pencil in your ideas on the 7 x 14 inch paper.

6. When your ink is dry, glue the calligraphy paper to the colored mounting paper. Glue the black strips to the top and bottom of the scroll. Add the string for hanging.

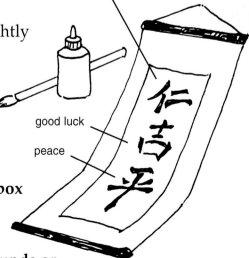

kindness

good luck

peace

There is evidence of writing in China 4000 years ago. The box containing the brush, ink and ink slab plus the paper is known as The Four Treasures of the Scholar's Studio. There are over 50,000 characters which represent things, sounds or ideas. There have been few changes so that today people can still read ancient texts.

MONGOLIAN RATTLE

A MONGOLIAN RATTLE

Materials: 2 paper bowls of any matching size, masking tape, drawing paper, 2 flat wooden craft sticks glued together, scissors, glue, colored markers, tempera or acrylic paints of any color, brushes, beans for the rattle sound, a variety of colored paper, bright ribbons.

1. Tape the bowl edges together, leaving an opening for inserting the beans and the handle of glued sticks.

2. Push the beans through the opening. Shake the rattle until you like the sound. Insert the handle and firmly wrap the masking tape around the handle, checking its firmness. It shouldn't wobble.

3. Cover the bowls with a layer of masking tape pieces. Paint the front and back of the rattle. Mongolians use a lot of red, turquoise and purple, yellow, bright pink, orange or chartreuse.

4. While the rattle is drying, using colored paper, make a face to glue on the flat part of the rattle. The traditional face is a monster face with symmetrical eyes, mouth and nose, big eyes, chin fringe and pointed ears. Sometimes the fringe was real fur, frayed silk, tassels or yarn pom-poms.

5. Perhaps another circle decoration can be made on the opposite rattle side. Dragons are common in Asian art.

6. Glue the monster face to the front of the rattle. Now add the finishing touches with patterns or dots on the edges. Tie the bright ribbons to the handle.

The Mongolian people have a strong musical heritage. They even claim that they "brought music to the world." The *hoomi* **mouth sounds of the herders are fluttering sounds that are both beautiful and strange. The herders' desire is to imitate the sounds of nature. Percussion objects such as rattles and a two-string cello-like instrument with a carved horse at the neck are part of the music of Mongolia.**

PAPER MAKING

THE ANCIENT CRAFT OF PAPER MAKING

Making paper with a blender: a blender, different scraps of colored and plain paper torn to about one inch, paper towels, shallow pan, teaspoon, Styrofoam meat tray, a piece of window screen about 8 x 8 inches, stapler, scissors, a cookie cutter or paper outline form, needle and thread.

1. First make a screen from the Styrofoam by cutting the center out with scissors. Save a 1 1/2 inch edge. Staple the screen around the edge keeping the top level. Trim screen edges.

2. To make the paper slurry fill the blender with 1 1/2 to 2 cups of hot water. Blend. The slurry should have lots of liquid. At this point add: dried or fresh herbs, tiny fresh flower petals or whole blossoms, glitter and bright pieces of ribbon, etc. Or the slurry can be poured into a cup and food coloring added to make colored slurry. It is fun to experiment.

3. Place the screen in the middle of the pan. Have the cookie cutter or paper outline ready. Spoon the paper slurry into the shape of the form. Press out the water with the back of the spoon. Make some colored paper slurry and put the color around the edges (see samples in the photograph). Press as much water out as possible. After the form has dried overnight gently remove from the screen and press on paper towel to remove all moisture.

4. If you make ornaments attach hanging loops with a needle and thread. Perhaps you had a greeting card in mind. You can make a lovely card by gluing your ornament on a prepared card of heavy paper that opens up to reveal your message.

Paper was invented nearly 2000 years ago in China. The inventor was T'sai Lun, an official of the Imperial Court. His thick sheets of paper were made from mulberry fibers, rags, fishnet parts, and hemp rope, all soaked in water and glue. Today the Japanese are considered to be the experts in creating fine paper. Paper is found in most areas of Japanese culture: architecture, fashion, art, sculpture, the food industry and packaging, to name only a few.

TIBETAN GONG

TIBETAN GONG

Materials: 7 bottling lids and rings, a total of 14 feet of cut cardboard strips that are 1 inch wide (these can be painted with red acrylic paint or use red railroad board) stapler and wire, bells, jewels or beads or tassels and a gold marker, the last five items being optional.

1. Cut your cardboard strips 1 inch wide. Cut 10 strips 13 inches long. These will be doubled as the 3 horizontal and 2 vertical center pieces.

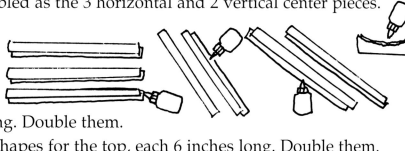

2. Cut 4 side
pieces 9 inches long. Double them.
Cut 2 decorative shapes for the top, each 6 inches long. Double them.

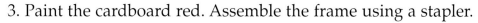

3. Paint the cardboard red. Assemble the frame using a stapler.

4. With a big nail and hammer (and the help of an adult), make a hole in each of the windows you have created, at the top, and in each of the rings or lids you want to attach.

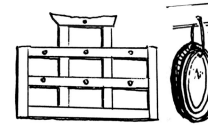

5. Push a piece of wire (about 3 inches) through the holes and attach the rings and lids.

6. Decorate the cardboard frame. You may add tassels at the corners. We added a touch of marker. Beads and bells decorate the black gong that uses aluminum cups.

Tibetan monks parade through the city streets playing these gongs as part of a religious celebration. They are wearing elaborate yellow head wear that is an ancient tradition. The Tibetan monks wear deep red robes.

SOUTHEAST ASIAN FOLK ART

This region blends its many folk arts in wood and stone carving, textiles, such as batik and woven designs, painting and puppet making. Bali, known for its fine art and craft traditions, takes its designs from natural forms and legendary figures.

SOUTHEAST ASIA

Many of the world's richest cultural traditions flourish in the small countries south of China in the Gulf of Thailand and the South China Sea. A blend of Hinduism, Buddhism and Confucianism religions, Christianity is a growing minor faith that has played an important historical role.

The border and political conflicts of the last 30 years found displaced Asians seeking refuge throughout the world. Many have come to the USA where the exposure and appreciation of their folk arts has enhanced our own cultural scene. Community festivals often include Hmong fiber art pieces, Malaysian music, Indonesian dancing and tasty foods from every country.

Myanmar (Burma)
Laos
Thailand
Vietnam
Cambodia
Philippines
Malaysia
Borneo
Java
Celebes
Bali
Indonesia

THAILAND: Tourism, important to the economy, has led to the development of some lost skills. Jim Thompson, an American in WW II revived the Thai silk industry which is now a leading export. The embroidery of the hill tribes such as Akha and Hmong have a zest for bold colors stitched against a dark cloth. After covering the surface with bright threads the artist will add beads, seeds, cowrie shells, silver coins and tassels of yarn, feathers or horsetail.

CAMBODIA:

This small country was originally settled by the Khmer 2000 years ago who drifted south from China. The ninth century is the golden age of Khmer kings with the building of the city Angkor with its temple honoring the Hindu faith. Angkor Wat was built in the twelfth century with Buddhist temples and sculptures added later. Thai forces invaded in 1500 and established the capital at Phnom Penh. Cambodians fled during the brutalities of the Khmer Rouge, communists who ruled in the eighties and are said to have killed a million people.

VIETNAM: It seems this land has been in conflict for most of its history. A part of French Indochina from the 1800s to World War II its independence was threatened by communism and civil war in the 1970's.

LAOS: Occupied by the French for fifty years Laos was impacted by the Vietnam War because the Ho Chi Minh trail went through the country. Refugees fled and migrated to other countries.

INDONESIA: These lands are the famed "East Indies" and "the Spice Islands" which the Europeans sought during the "Age of Discovery." Much of the area was dominated by the Dutch. Spread out over 13,000 islands, Indonesia has jungles, desert, mountains and rice fields. 350 different ethnic cultures have lived on the islands for hundreds of years. Bali is especially well-known for its crafts and beauty. The batiks of Java are the world's finest. The word "batik" means to "create with dots." Delicate designs are achieved with a pen-like tool that controls the hot wax. Waxing, dyeing and boiling out the wax is a process that could be repeated 20 times. East Sumba is known for its ikat weaving as this is another fiber skill that might take months to finish. Balinese dance is charged with energy. The bright, darting eyes, high stepping, raised arms, quick cat-like movements take years for the young dancers to perfect.

creating a batik

a Legong dancer

hand-made umbrellas

a Bali carving

MALAYSIA: This country is two lands divided by 400 miles of water, the China Sea. Tourism brochures claim."only Malaysia has it all". The split country features unexplored tropical forests, traditional fishing villages, beaches and fine crafts.

THE PHILIPPINES: The Spanish colonized this archipelago of 7,000 islands in the 1500s and named them after King Philip of Spain. The imprint is so strong that Filipinos are sometimes called "Asian Latinos." Much of the island area is hallowed ground to World War II veterans who served under Douglas MacArthur and experienced heavy battle and the Bataan Death March of l942. In 1946 the country became independent. The folk art traditions reflect the mix of Malays, Indonesians and Chinese that live there today.

A THAI SPIRIT HOUSE

A Thai Spirit House

Materials: a fat rectangular box (we used a pop tart box), manila file folder, tempera paint in Thai traditional colors: purple, yellow, chartreuse, orange, scissors, pencil, big brushes, glue, cardboard platform for the house.

1. Paint the emptied box until the printing is covered (this may take several coats, or spray paint it first and then paint with tempera).

2. For the roof, lay the folder flat. Cut it the width of the box and at least 12 inches long. Fold the roof cardboard in half and see if it creates a peaked pitch (A). Measure each end for the four decorative "carved" pieces (B) and the two triangular end pieces (C).

3. Using this pattern cut out the four carved units. Paint them a contrasting color on both sides. Fold the flaps and glue them to the 4 sides of the roof ends. Cut out 2 finials (D), paint on both sides and put aside.

4. Fold the roof and pencil the triangle end pieces to fit. Add 1 inch tabs for gluing. Cut out two end triangles and paint them and the roof a color.

5. Glue the tabbed triangle ends to the roof and glue the entire roof onto the box/house. Finally glue the carved spires on either end. Decorate the roof and the house. Mount the little house on the cardboard platform.

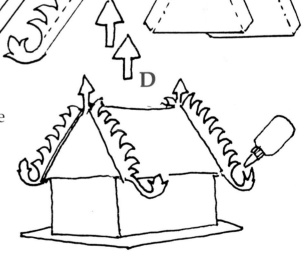

Thais build these small colorful houses for the spirit of *Phi*, and place offerings outside. Some look like small temples and are fancy. Others are models of real houses. Thai people believe the spirits that guard a place live in the spirit house. Every day people bring the spirits food and flowers.

HMONG CAP

HMONG CAP

Materials: 2 pieces of 8 1/2 x 11 inch graph paper with 1/4 inch squares, a piece of black railroad board 14 x 24 inch, fine-tipped markers of multiple colors, ruler, pencil, scissors, 2 bright circles of paper, one 7 inch circle, a 4 1/2 inch circle, stapler and glue.

1. Pencil five 4 x 4 inch squares onto the graph paper. Draw a circle that is 3 1/2 inches in circumference. Make 2 triangles cut from a 3 x 3 inch square. Here are some Hmong patterns traditionally done with colorful embroidery but in grided squares of cloth instead of paper. See Hmong design ideas on page 83.

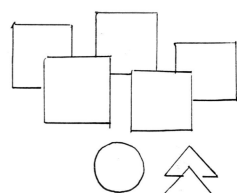

2. Cut the hat pattern from the black railroad board to look like this:

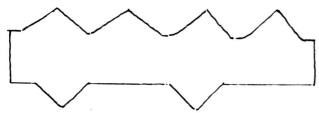

3. Glue the graph paper squares to your flat strip, putting the triangle shapes on the flaps. Save the decorated circle graph design. Join the two ends and staple them securely (A). Join the four peaks by bending them toward the center and staple the tips. Cover the hat top with this decorated circle piece.

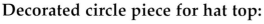

Decorated circle piece for hat top:
a. Cut around the biggest paper circle making fringe 1/8" cuts. Then do the same to the smaller circle.
b. Glue the graph circle (B) over the fringe of the small circle which is glued on top of the bigger circle. Now glue the unfringed layered circle to the top of the hat, centering it.

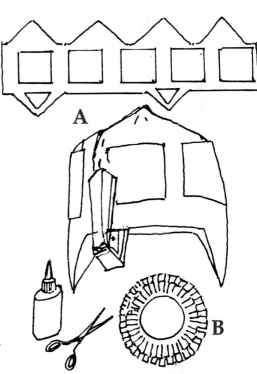

Try your paper Hmong hat on. Center the ear flaps over your ears. This beautiful cap should be big enough for the average head.

Hmong mothers always gave lavish design to the children's caps they made. The top was made to look like a lovely flower. It was believed that bad spirits would mistake the hat tops for blossoms and bypass them as they flew by.

FESTIVE DELIGHT FROM INDONESIA

FESTIVE DELIGHT FROM INDONESIA

Materials: A strip of railroad board 6 x 18 inches long, a big-eyed needle, yarn, string, scissors, embroidery floss etc., random big-holed beads, colorful paper or fabric scraps, foil, pasta (plain or painted) nearly anything bright that can be strung.

1. The circle hoops that give this piece its form can be strips of cardboard, or any stiff material you may have on hand.

2. Assemble the beads, cut strips of paper or cloth 4 to 6 inches long, cut shiny shapes out of stiff silver and gold paper, color your pasta etc.

3. The first hoop is 15 inches in diameter. Punch holes with a scissors tip, laying the 15 inch strip on a cushioned surface. Punch the holes one inch apart. Glue or sew the ends and secure with a paper clip (it is much easier to push the threaded needle through the pre-punched holes).

4. Start with 8 yarn strands, each about 12 inches long. Gather the thread tops and thread through two or three 1/2 inch holed beads. Threading each yarn through the needle, string paper strips, beads, etc. and pull thread through **every other punched hole**.

5. Make the second hoop about 22 inches long. Punch holes three inches apart. The seven yarn lengths are each 24 inches. Thread the knotted yarn through the top ring hole, string beads and decorative pieces on the thread. Thread through the holes and continue adding decorative pieces, putting a bauble on the yarn end. Secure each end of the strings securely with strong knots or a double loop through the cardboard ring hole. Make a hanging loop at the top and suspend it to add a festive touch to an event.

Indonesian people, though they are of many origins, are skilled with their hands and especially creative with simple materials. The tradition of creating a festive, colorful environment originated with old royal courts where the national dance, Legong can be traced. The gamelan orchestra of metal gongs and flutes is part of Indonesia's early musical heritage. Elaborate, hanging decorative pieces are part of that early practice.

BATIK TECHNIQUE

BATIK TECHNIQUE

Materials: cotton or near-cotton blends that are cut to the desired size, flour and alum (from the spice section) and a container for mixing, a plastic squeeze bottle with a small hole funnel, pencil for composing design, waxed paper, black marker and masking tape, acrylic paint, a large bristled brush, sudsy water and spatula for removing dried paste.

1. See page 83 for traditional batik design ideas.

2. Draw the design in pencil on a piece of paper cut the same size as your cloth.

A.

3. Go over the penciled designs with a heavy dark marker.

4. Put drawing on surface first. Then tape waxed paper over it and the fabric over the waxed paper (A). You have three layers.

5. Make the flour, water and alum paste. Here is the recipe:

Paste Batik Recipe
Mix into a blender or a bowl:
1/2 cup of water • 2 teaspoons alum • 1/2 cup of flour

6. After mixing, pour into a plastic squeeze bottle. Try to use paste the same day it is mixed. Practice the thickness of your lines by squirting gently on a newspaper. Practice "drawing" with the tip.

7. Once you have regulated the paste line, start applying the paste to your design. The parts covered by the paste will not have paint. Let the paste dry overnight.

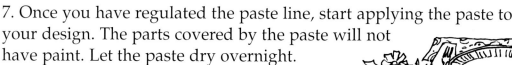

8. Brush on the paint. Cover all of the surface you want colored. Let the paint *thoroughly* dry.

9. Put the batiked fabric into a sink of soapy water and gently scrape the dry paste off the fabric. This will leave a mess in the sink so be prepared for clean up. Dry the fabric for a final time. How are the results? Here are some ideas on how to use your batik fabric in a traditional way: as gift wrap, a place mat, a pillow.

The Indian influence on Indonesian arts is strong except for a few truly indigenous arts: batik, the shadow theater, gamelan music, and metalworking techniques. The patterns and unusually rich use of batik has made Bali and other Indonesian regions famous for their textiles.

HMONG POUCH

HMONG POUCH

Materials: white craft paper 15 x 13 inches,1/4 inch graph paper, 8 small washers (hardware store), fine-tipped markers or colored pencils, pencil, ruler, scissors, strong glue, strip for band 24 x 4 inches.

1. Cut the paper bag parts A and B. Glue the body of the bag together allowing for two inches at the bottom for cut fringe.

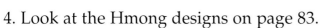

2. Cut the graph paper a size that will cover the front of the bag. Cut two joined triangles from the graph paper for the flap decoration.

4. Look at the Hmong designs on page 83. After studying the Hmong designs choose 4 or 5 and select your 7or 8 colors of fine-tipped markers. Use the ruler and the grid paper to mark off a symmetrical design. The Hmongs would use embroidery thread. We are substituting markers or colored pencils to make the design.

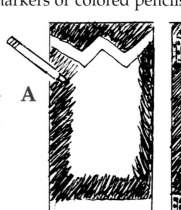

5. Using a dominant color, color the bag around the edges before gluing the graph paper design onto the white paper parts (A). Color the graph paper square with the Hmong design. Color the triangles too. Now glue the graph paper design on the paper bag colored brightly around the edges.

6. Clip the paper fringe. Add the dots of color that represent small beads (B).

7. Glue the washers to the finished fringe on the flap and the bottom of the bag.

8 Glue the edges and create a 24" strip. Color the strip with Hmong designs. Glue the two band ends to the back of the bag. Glue on a line of washers up the body of the strip.

This pretty purse is a traditional part of the costume of White Hmong women from north central Laos. A full costume may have a purse in back and two more worn on either side. The bags are meant to be symbolic rather than useful.

INDONESIAN MASK

INDONESIAN MASK

Materials: white railroad board 10 x10 inches, scissors, markers in black, red, blue, aqua, and yellow.

1. Cut out the white mask form using the pattern. Cut out the nose piece. Fold the face in half and place on the face of the wearer. Is it the correct fit? Lightly mark the place for the nose and eyes with a pencil.

2. Cut the slots for the nose tabs and insert them, securing the nose tabs by taping them to the mask back.

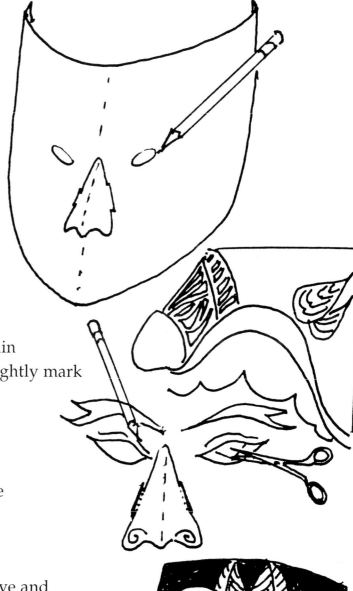

3. Paint on the exotic eyes and brows. Again measure the mask on the wearer's face. Lightly mark the eye hole places once more to be sure. Cut out the eye holes.

4. Marker or crayon in the black hair, gold decoration and wing-like decoration in the hair center. Your colors should be strong, vibrant and sharp.

5. Color in the mouth. Use the following eye and mouth design suggestions.

6. Add string on either side for the wearing of the mask.

The Indonesian masked dance tradition (*wayang topeng*) is strongest in Java and Bali and closely allied to Javanese puppet plays. The dancers angular movements, flamboyant costumes and painted wooden face masks mimic the smaller puppets (*wayang golek*).

ASIAN SHADOW PUPPETS

ASIAN SHADOW PUPPET

Materials: a 6 to 8 inch gold doily, manila folder 8 1/2 x 11 inches, 4 brads, scissors, pencil, black and red markers, 2 sticks, 6 inches long, (or two taped together), glue, a hole punch, masking tape and the pattern page 79.

The unusual appearance of the shadow puppet is achieved by exaggeration. The long, sharp nose and chin, the tall headpiece are typical of their appearance. So are the very long arms with crescent-tapered hands and long curved fingernails. The toes are often turned up.

1. Copy the puppet page pattern. Lay it out on your folder. Transfer the pieces by tracing around the cutouts or use a carbon paper technique.

2. Pencil in the features and the places you will cut out. Cut out the areas for the doily (A). Marker or crayon with black the cardboard outlines, the hair and face. Add the few red touches.

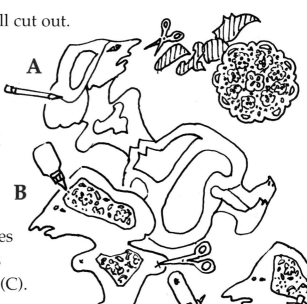

3. Put the gold doily behind the cutout places. You will have to cut the doily into pieces to fill up the empty sections (B).

4. Make holes with a scissors point at the places marked on the arm pattern pieces. Push brads through the holes and attach to the shoulders (C).

5. Attach the long stick to the back of the puppet with masking tape. Attach the short sticks to the hands with slender strips of masking tape.

6. Place a light in front of the puppet and watch its shadow. Use the sticks to give the puppet motion and life.

These earliest lacy puppets are thought to have their origin in China. Their popularity spread to Southeast Asia and have been performed in Java for 1000 years. They are called *Wayang Kulit (wand coo lit).* **wayan meaning shadow and kulit meaning skin. The largest puppets are ogres and symbolize gross habits, violent natures, big noses, round eyes and heavy bodies. They are always defeated by the smaller, pretty and spiritually superior heroes. These have slim, small heads, bent faces that look down delicate narrow noses to fine lips.**

PAPER CHAINS

PAPER CHAINS

Materials: large sheet of brightly colored paper (such as butcher paper, construction paper, wrapping paper, or wallpaper), scissors, pencil, sponge or rag, water-based paint, tray for paint, glue or tape, patterns on page 82.

1. Cut the paper into strips 5 to 7 inches wide and as long as possible.

2. Fold the strip accordion-style into 3 or 4 sections. Cut off any excess paper.

3. Choose a pattern from pages 82.

4. With your pencil, trace the pattern from our pattern page or design your own. Make certain that some part of the design extends at least to the folded sides so that when it is cut out the shapes will be connected.

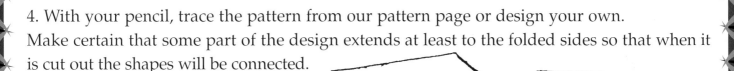

5. If you want to paint the paper with a sponge, do so and let the paint dry. Fold the strip again and cut out the shape you have drawn. To keep the layers of paper from sliding around while you cut, staple or paper clip the layers together on the part of your paper that will be cut away.

6. Repeat as desired until you have several strips. Fasten together the parts of your paper chain using glue or tape.

Tips for cutting paper chains:
- Good papers for cutting are origami-printed papers, quality bond paper, decorative gift wrap, wallpaper from sample books, and construction paper.
- Construction paper may be too bulky to cut when folded to more than two thicknesses.
- Paper clips or staples will hold the folds in place while you cut your chains.
- An adult can help you cut small areas with a utility knife.

Tips for sponge-painting your paper chains:
- Fill a shallow tray with paint. Touch your sponge onto the surface of the paint-filled tray and *lightly* daub your laid out paper. Let it dry before folding. Try more than one color of paint.

JAPANESE CARP KITE

a celebration of Children's Day

Materials: 24" x 36" piece of butcher paper (any color), tissue paper scraps, 1" x 24" cardboard strip or 24" piece of wire, glue, scissors, stapler, markers, crepe paper or ribbon for streamers, hole punch, 3 1-foot lengths of string, long pole (optional).

1. First fold over 1" of the short side of your tissue paper. Place your 24" strip of wire, or cardboard in the fold and glue.

2. Next fold your tissue paper in half the long way. Glue it along the edge with a small amount of glue. Let dry.

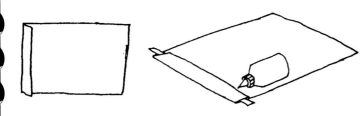

3. Insert a folded newspaper between the tissue sheets to protect the underside. With the markers draw and color in the shape of a large fish. The mouth will be near the end with the fold.

4. Glue on tissue paper fish scales, fins, eyes, gills, etc. from the tissue scraps. Add long streamers on the tail if you wish.

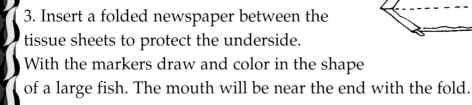

5. Bend the wire or cardboard to form an open circle at the mouth end of your kite. Staple the cardboard to strengthen the circle.

6. Tie on the 3 strings to the "mouth" of your kite and attach to a long pole. Hang outside on a bright sunny day.

On May 5, Japan celebrates Tango-no-seku, traditionally Boy's Day but now adopted as Children's Day: Kodomo-no-hi. Carp banners are flown from rooftops with each fish representing the number of sons in the family. It is common for boys to do a display of warrior implements and dolls. A special bean cake is eaten and parents give thanks for their healthy sons. The carp is a symbol of courage, power and determination, as it swims against the current. Small boys crawl through the paper carp kites from mouth to tail. If the paper is not torn or punctured the child will have good luck.

JAPANESE PAPER DOLLS

for everyone to do at Hina Matsuri

Materials: colored copy paper or origami patterned paper (1/2 sheet, 5 1/2" x 8 1/2"), scissors, glue, markers, paper scraps.

1. Cut your sheet of paper in half as shown.

2. Cut a small head shape about the size of a quarter with a long neck from a scrap piece of paper. Draw facial features with a pencil. Save until later.

3. A) Take one of your pieces of paper. Cut 1/2" strip off the long edge.
   B) Fold the top edge of this paper over twice.
   C) Turn this over so that the folds are on the back. Locate the center and fold both top corners to the center as shown making the neckline of the kimono. Leave a small space in the neckline to hold your head shape.
   D) Fold each side in again, lining up the bottom edges as you fold. If one side sticks out simply cut it off.

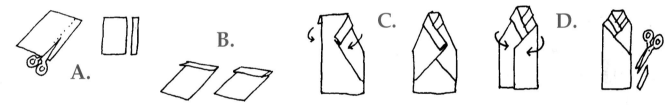

4. Take the 1/2" strip from step 3 and wrap it around the waist beginning in the front. Either glue or fold under in the back. Insert the head.

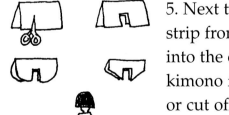

5. Next take another sheet of paper to make the sleeves. Cut off a 1" strip from the short edge. Fold the larger piece in half. Cut a rectangle into the center of the open edges (no larger than kimono form). Round off each edge for a girl's kimono or cut off angular straight sleeves for a boy's. Glue onto back of kimono with open slit down.

Hina Matsuri is Japanese Girl's Day in Japan and is also Doll Festival Day. It is a holiday when parents express their love and pride in their daughters.

During Hina Matsuri girls wear their best kimonos and hold a tea ceremony with invited girls and their dolls. All are very polite and have proper manners as they enjoy the sweet rice cakes in colors of green, pink and white.

Welcoming Cat

continued from Good Luck Toys on page 16.

Materials: a toilet paper cardboard tube, half of the recipe of cooked play dough on page 79, white, red, black, yellow and green acrylic or tempera paint, a fine-tip brush, a broad-tip brush, pencil and a container of water.

1. You will need a ball of cooked salt dough the size of a big orange. Save another ball the size of a lime for ears, arm and details.

2. Holding the cardboard tube, mold the big ball of dough around it. The head will be molded over the top of the hollow cardboard cylinder. With four finger-size clay "worms" form the cat legs and haunches, the resting arm, the nose, cheeks and ears. Dip your fingertips into the water and smooth the rough edges of the body parts. The hollow tube should be seen when you tip the cat upside down.

3. Finally add the waving arm with the tipped paw. Use the water to smooth the arm into the cat body.

4. Let the sculpture dry in a sunny (but not excessively hot) place for 24 hours. When you can feel the clay "give" under the dried surface it is not thoroughly dry. Allow more drying time.

Painting the cat:

1. Brush white paint on the sculpture. Let it thoroughly dry. Add another coat if your cat is not white.

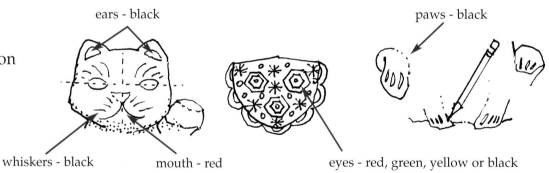

ears - black

paws - black

whiskers - black

mouth - red

eyes - red, green, yellow or black

2. With a pencil carefully mark the eyes, nose, mouth, whiskers, bib and claws. The bib can be creative and have your own design. All the cats follow a stylized formula in colors and form.

3. Before painting, check that your penciled features are symmetrical. Place the edge of a piece of paper down its middle. Except for the resting paw and the waving paw, the features should be the same on both half sides. Using the fine-tipped brush and the red, black and optional colors paint in the cat details.

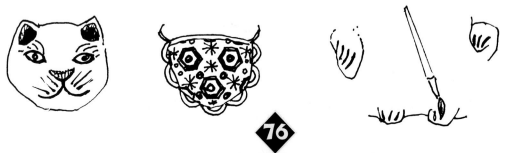

JAPANESE NO MASK

Continued from page 23.

Materials: a piece of heavy paper 8"x 12", sponge, brown, yellow, white tempera paint, strong black marker, scissors, pencil, stapler, string, paper plate,

1. Look at the mask in the photograph on page 22. By enlarging this pattern you can draw the eyes, nostrils and mouth. Cut them out with your scissors.

2. Wet your sponge on a corner. Put about a finger tip blob of each paint color on a paper plate. Dip the sponge into the white with a dab of brown and sponge-paint your face mask. Adding a mix of brown and yellow (you want to have the mask resemble carved wood) sponge a dark section around the lower half of the face and above the eyebrows.

3. After your paint has dried add the black marker accents of eyebrows, eye-liner and the whiskers.

4. Put the mask up to the face of the wearer and determine the best place to attach the string for wearing the mask. Staple or tie the string on.

(You may do a variation of this mask with its simple eyes and mouth. You can make it colorful or dark and evil appearing. We have made our mask to resemble the museum mask that is old and authentic).

The earliest No dramas were performed 600 years ago. They were considered so sacred they were performed only for the gods. Later nobility and samurai were allowed to attend. It is only in recent times that the public has seen the plays. The No stage has not changed: four pillars mark the stage, the main figure called "Shite" is joined by Waki and a chorus. The Waki tells the story, comments on the plot and often explains it to the audience and even mediates with the gods. Performances are usually a day long event, broken up with comedians called Kyogen as well as dances by the chorus.

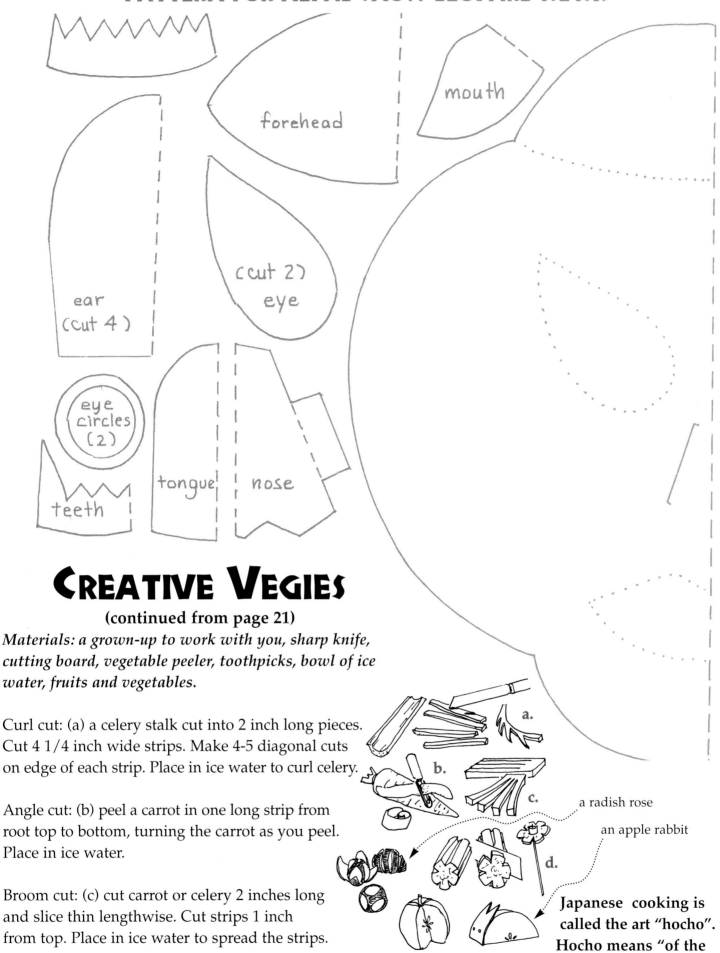

forehead

mouth

ear
(cut 4)

(cut 2)
eye

eye
circles
(2)

teeth

tongue

nose

CREATIVE VEGIES

(continued from page 21)

Materials: a grown-up to work with you, sharp knife, cutting board, vegetable peeler, toothpicks, bowl of ice water, fruits and vegetables.

Curl cut: (a) a celery stalk cut into 2 inch long pieces. Cut 4 1/4 inch wide strips. Make 4-5 diagonal cuts on edge of each strip. Place in ice water to curl celery.

Angle cut: (b) peel a carrot in one long strip from root top to bottom, turning the carrot as you peel. Place in ice water.

Broom cut: (c) cut carrot or celery 2 inches long and slice thin lengthwise. Cut strips 1 inch from top. Place in ice water to spread the strips.

Flower cut: (d) for carrot, turnip or beet. Cut V shapes around a 2 inch piece. Slice into flowers, skewer and add green pea or lemon rind centers.

a.

b.

c.

a radish rose

an apple rabbit

d.

Japanese cooking is called the art "hocho". Hocho means "of the knife." It is the art of carving the freshest, prettiest food to please our appetite and our eyes. Beautifully cut fruits and vegetables as garnishes are a special part of "hocho".

PATTERN FOR SHADOW PUPPET

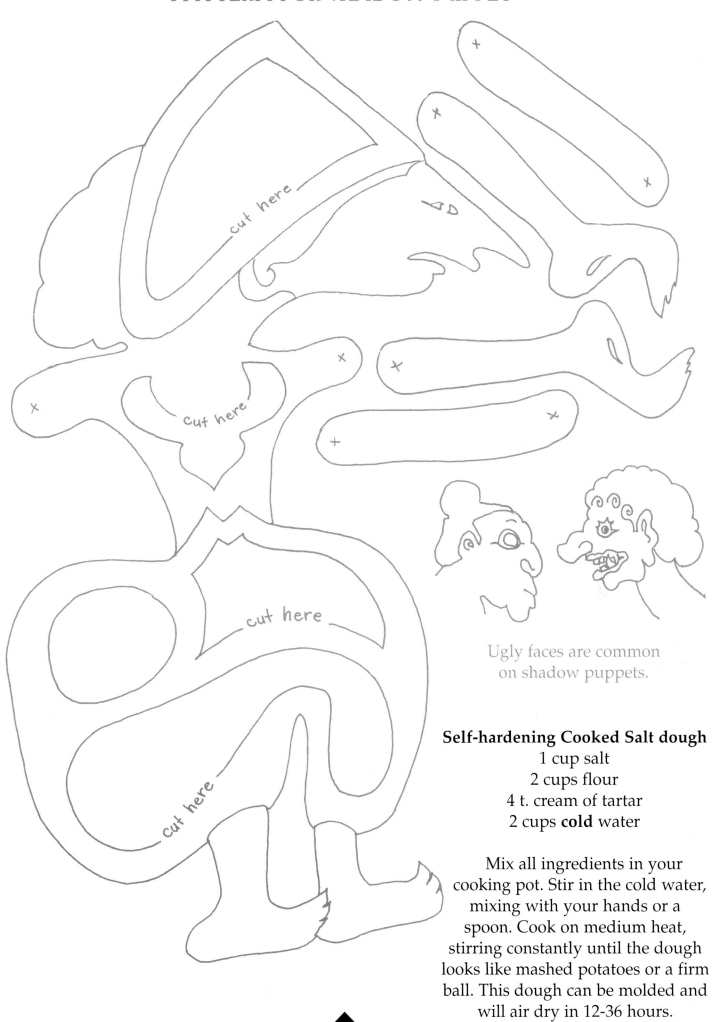

cut here

cut here

cut here

cut here

cut here

Ugly faces are common
on shadow puppets.

Self-hardening Cooked Salt dough
1 cup salt
2 cups flour
4 t. cream of tartar
2 cups **cold** water

Mix all ingredients in your
cooking pot. Stir in the cold water,
mixing with your hands or a
spoon. Cook on medium heat,
stirring constantly until the dough
looks like mashed potatoes or a firm
ball. This dough can be molded and
will air dry in 12-36 hours.

SHINTO BIRD

continued from page 31.

Materials: a cardboard tube 4 to 8 inches long, white paper, glue, scissors, black paper, red and black markers.

1. The bird can be the tube's natural brown or cover the tube with white paper.

2. Cut notches around the top of the tube, each about 1/2 inch wide(A). Fold these into the tube center. Cut out two black circles about 1 1/2 inches wide. Make a cut to the center and fold the edges under so the black paper makes a shallow dish (B). Glue it to the top of the cylinder and the folded-in edges.

3. Make the bird feathers by rolling 1/4 inch cut strips around a pencil (this is called "quilling"). Make at least 25 rolls. Glue one and two to the stem of the third quill(C). After all the quills have been glued insert them around the black cap and glue them down (D). Now cut, glue and place the second black paper cap over the first (E).

4. Marker on the eyes, claws and the traditional red beak.

These charming birds are traditionally carved from a soft wood. The feathers are curls of wood. They are commonly found at Shinto shrines. Shintoism reveres nature and believes in kami, spirits that live in all natural things. These carved birds were part of shrine ceremonies honoring birds.

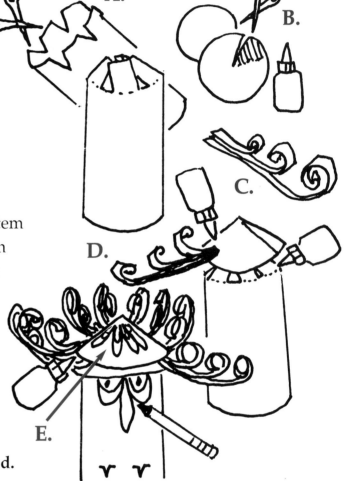

A.

B.

C.

D.

E.

CULTURAL PATTERNS

JAPAN

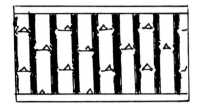
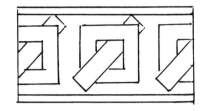

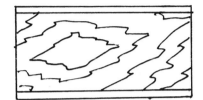

CHINA

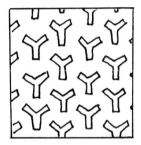

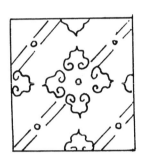

INDONESIA

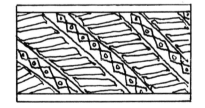

HMONG

INDEX

ACKNOWLEDGMENTS

Nancy Weiser, the Kimono Lady, shared her rare Japanese fiber pieces
and fine collectibles for the photographs. Her expertise and generosity are appreciated.
Kay Jones shared many of her Asian pieces for the photographs and
gave excellent advice on most aspects of the book.
Emily Mortensen edited, corrected, improved the text and instructions.
Annie Hatch of the Utah Folk Art Museum loaned handcrafted pieces
from the collection.
Jean Irwin of the Utah Arts Council, Multicultural Specialist,
assisted with the choice of activities in the Japanese section.
Jean also edited and corrected much of that section.
Madlyn Tanner edited the manuscript.
Aida Santos-Mattingly of the Filippino Performing Arts helped
arrange Filippino dancers for the title page photo.

A special thanks to Rachel R. Treslar for sharing her experiences and
carefully chosen objects from her years in Korea.
Thank you to the Vietnamese Volunteer Youth Association
Nhu Uyer Phan, Doan-Ouynh Phan and Te Van Phan:
Leader of Vietnamese Volunteer Association
Additional appreciation to:
Rita Suyoto and Anna Pratt: Indonesian community
Jung Hee Lovejoy Korean American community and
Karma and Sonom Sok-Choekore
Tibetan weaving

BIBLIOGRAPHY

1. Simpson, Penny, Lucy Kitto, Kanji Sodeoka, The Japanese Pottery Handbook, Kodansha International Ltd., Tokyo, 1979.

2. The Folk Arts of Japan, The Japan Society, Inc., N.Y., Minsterberg, Hugo, Charles E Tuttle Company, Tokyo, Japan.

3. St. Tamara Kolba, Asian Crafts, The Lion Press, N.Y., 1970.

4. Maarein, Shirley, Oriental Images, Viking Press, New York, New York, 1978

5. Temko, Florence, Folk Crafts for World Friendship, Doubleday and Company, Inc., Garden City, New York, 1976.

6. Los Angeles Mask Theater, International Mask Research Foundation, Santa Monica, California, 1979.

7. MacDowell, Marsha, Folk Arts Curator, Hmong Folk Arts: A Guide for Teachers, The Museum, Michigan State University, East Lansing, Michigan.

8. Baker, Muriel and Lunt, Margaret, Blue And White: The Cotton Embroideries of Rural China, Charles Scribner, New York, 1977.

9. Munsterberg, Hugo, The Folk Arts of Japan, Charles E. Tuttle Company, Tokyo, Japan, 1958.

10. Hauge, Victor and Takako, Folk Traditions in Japanese Art, Kodansha International Ltd., Tokyo, 1978.

11. Glubok, Shirley, The Art of Japan, Macmillan Co., NYC. 1970.

12. John Michael Kohler Arts Center, Hmong Art: Tradition and Change, Sheboygan Arts Foundation, Sheboygan, Wis., 1986.

13. Mallinson, Donnelly and Hang, H'mong Batik, Univ. of Washington Press, Seattle, Wash., 1988.

14. Zhang, Song Nan, The Children of China, An Artist's Journey, Tundra Books, Montreal, Canada, 1995.

15. Nicholson, Robert and Watts, Claire, Ancient China, A Journey into Civilization series, Chelsea House Publishers, New York, 1994.

16. Russell, William, Taiwan, Islands in the Sea, The Rourke Book Company, Vero Beach, Florida, 1994.

17. Cotterell, Arthur, Ancient China, Eyewitness Books, Alfred A. Knopf, New York, London, 1994.

18. Hmong Art Tradition and Change, John Michael Kohler Arts Center, Sheboygan, Wisconsin, 1986.

19. Kindersley, Barnabas and Anabel, Celebrations! Children Just Like Me, DK Publishing, London, 1997.

20. Civilizations of Asia, Raintree Publishing, Milwaukee, Wis.,1989.

21. Herald, Jacqueline, World Crafts, Lark Books, Asheville, N.C., 1992.

22. Baten, Lea, Japanese Folk Toys: The Playful Arts, Shufunotomo, Japan, 1992.

23. Oka, Hideyuki, How to Wrap Five Eggs: Traditional Japanese Packaging, Weatherhill, Inc., Tokyo, 1967.

24. Oka, Hideyuki, How to Wrap Five More Eggs, Weatherhill, Tokyo, 1975.

25. Kenneway, Eric, Complete Origami, St. Martin's, Griffin, New York, 1987.

26. Takahama, Toshie, The Complete Origami Collection, Shufunomoto Co., Tokyo, 1997.

27. Harbin, Robert, The Secrets of Origami: The Japanese Art of Paper Folding, Dover Publications, Inc., 1997.

28. Kokko, Margo, The Final Touch: Decorating Garnishes, CBI Publishing Co., Boston, Mass., 1982.

29. Paz, Octavio, In Praise of Hands, World Crafts Council, New York Graphic Society, Greenwich, Connecticut, 1974.

30. Stack, Peggy Fletcher, A World of Faith, Signature Books, Salt Lake City, UT, 1998.

Hands-on Alaska
(ISBN 0-9643177-3-7)

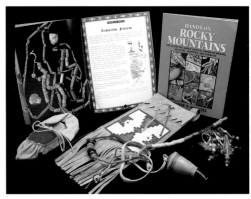

Hands-on Rocky Mountains
(ISBN 0-9643177-2-9)

Books from
KITS PUBLISHING

Hands-on Latin America
(ISBN 0-9643177-1-0)

Consider these book for:

the library

teaching social studies

art

multicultural programs

ESL programs

museum programs

community youth events

home enrichment

Hands-on Celebrations
(ISBN 0-9643177-4-5)

Hands-on Pioneers
(ISBN 1-57345-085-5)

Hands-on Asia
(ISBN 0-9643177-5-3)

ORDER FORM

SEND TO:_____ PO # _____

ADDRESS:_____

CITY:_____ STATE:_____ ZIP_____

CONTACT NAME: _____ PHONE: _____

❒ ____ Hands-on Asia

❒ ____ Hands-on Latin America

❒ ____ Hands-on Rocky Mountains

❒ ____ Hands-on Pioneers

❒ ____ Hands-on Celebrations

❒ ____ Hands-on Alaska

_____ Total Quantity Ordered

_____ Shipping and Handling

_____ Total Enclosed/PO

Books are $20⁰⁰ each.
Shipping and Handling - $3⁰⁰ for the first book
  and $1⁰⁰ for each additional book.
All books shipped book rate unless otherwise requested.

Make checks payable to:
KITS PUBLISHING
2359 E. Bryan Avenue
Salt Lake City, Utah 84108
1-801-582-2517 fax: (801) 582-2540
e-mail - info@hands-on.com

CHINA

1. Tibetan carpet
2. Woven Yak hair harness from Mongolia
3. Tibetan brass singing bowl
4. Chinese embroidered child's hat
5. Chinese embroidered jacket
6. Chinese dolls
7. Chinese slippers
8. Chinese pin cushion with people in a circle
9. Chinese embroidered box
10. Chinese place mat with embroidery
11. Korean dolls
12. Korean wedding ducks
13. Korean celadon vase
14. Korean small carved ducks
15. Korean pendant
16. Korean textile
17. Korean wrapper
18. Korean wooden mask
19. Twirling drum from China
20. Chinese wooden tray with tassel

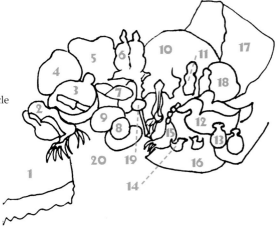

CHINA

SOUTHEAST ASIA

1. Burmese ivory temple
2. Indonesian carved goddess
3. Burmese carved ivory figures
4. Akha belt
5. Cambodian hat
6. Akha headwear
7. Dyed feather Akha cape
8. Cambodian hat
9. Laotian drum
10. Javanese tea set
11. Woven Vietnamese cloth
12. Woven Vietnamese cloth
13. Karen hill tribe jacket
14. Hmong fabric
15. Burmese temple bells
16 Ikat textile from Indonesia

SOUTHEAST ASIA

JAPAN

1. Japanese painting
2. Japanese doll for Hina Matsuri
3. Doll for Hina Matsuri
4. Silk fan
5. clogs
6. daruma
7. paper ball
8. doll
9. miniature pagoda
10. fan
11. Noh mask
12. woven sandwich carrier
13. ceramic tray
14. horse
15. fork
16. kokeshi doll
17. welcoming cat
18. grass sushi mat
19. men's clog
20. calligraphy scroll
21. wooden scoop

JAPAN

Asian Endsheets

1. Carved goddess statue from Thailand
2. Mask from Indonesia
3. Frog mask from Indonesia
4. Bronze Hindu statue
5. Hmong applique and embroidered textiles
6. Laotian elephant mask
7. Hmong ornaments
8. Painting from Java
9. Akha Hill tribe woman's headwear
10. Carvings from Bali

ASIAN ENDSHEETS

980-3